HAL•LEONARD
INSTRUMENTAL
PLAY-ALONG

ALTO SAX

PIRATES OF THE CARIBBEAN

ISBN-13: 978-1-4234-2197-9
ISBN-10: 1-4234-2197-3

WALT DISNEY MUSIC COMPANY

DISTRIBUTED BY

HAL•LEONARD®
CORPORATION
7777 W. BLUEMOUND RD. P.O. BOX 13819 MILWAUKEE, WI 53213

Visit Hal Leonard Online at
www.halleonard.com

◆ THE BLACK PEARL

ALTO SAX

Music by KLAUS BADELT

small notes optional

p

❷ BLOOD RITUAL/
MOONLIGHT SERENADE

ALTO SAX

Music by KLAUS BADELT

◆ DAVY JONES PLAYS HIS ORGAN

ALTO SAX

Music by HANS ZIMMER

❸ DAVY JONES

ALTO SAX

Music by HANS ZIMMER

◆ DINNER IS SERVED

ALTO SAX

Music by HANS ZIMMER

7 I'VE GOT MY EYE ON YOU

ALTO SAX

Music by HANS ZIMMER

◆ HE'S A PIRATE

ALTO SAX

Music by KLAUS BADELT

◆ JACK SPARROW

ALTO SAX

Music by HANS ZIMMER

◆⑨ THE KRAKEN

ALTO SAX

Music by HANS ZIMMER

⑩ THE MEDALLION CALLS

ALTO SAX

Music by KLAUS BADELT

⬥ ONE LAST SHOT

ALTO SAX

Music by KLAUS BADELT

◆12 TO THE PIRATE'S CAVE!

ALTO SAX

Music by KLAUS BADELT

⑬ TWO HORNPIPES
(Fisher's Hornpipe)

ALTO SAX

By SKIP HENDERSON

15 WHEEL OF FORTUNE

ALTO SAX

Music by HANS ZIMMER

⬥ UNDERWATER MARCH

ALTO SAX

Music by KLAUS BADELT